THE POCKET

PEMA CHÖDRÖN

THE POCKET

PEMA CHÖDRÖN

EDITED BY

Eden Steinberg

SHAMBHALA · Boulder · 2017

Shambhala Publications, Inc.
4720 Walnut Street
Boulder, Colorado 80301
www.shambhala.com

9 8 7 6 5 4 3 2 1

Printed in the United States of America

♾ This edition is printed on acid-free paper that meets the
American National Standards Institute z39.48 Standard.
♻ This book is printed on 30% postconsumer recycled paper.
For more information please visit us at www.shambhala.com.

Distributed in the United States by Penguin Random House LLC
and in Canada by Random House of Canada Ltd

Designed by Lora Zorian

The Library of Congress catalogues
the previous editon of this book as follows:

Chödrön, Pema.
The pocket Pema Chödrön.—1st ed.
p.   cm.
ISBN 978-1-59030-651-2 (pbk.: alk. paper)
ISBN 978-1-61180-442-3 (Shambhala Pocket Library)
1. Religious life—Buddhism.   I. Title.
BQ5405.C46 2008
294.3'444—dc22
2008017612

CONTENTS

EDITOR'S PREFACE

This collection brings together some of the most memorable, pithy, and potent teachings of Pema Chödrön, the beloved American Buddhist nun and best-selling author. Drawn from her previously published works, these teachings offer us a bold vision of meeting each moment of our lives with greater wisdom, courage, and compassion.

Pema Chödrön has a stunning gift for expressing the Buddhist teachings in straightforward terms that resonate with people's lived experience—a gift born of more than three decades of committed study and practice of Tibetan Buddhism.

Many of her readers may not know that she was born Deirdre Blomfield-Brown in New York and began studying Tibetan Buddhism in 1972. She was ordained as a nun in 1974, at the age of thirty-eight. For thirteen years she studied with the renowned Tibetan meditation master Chögyam Trungpa, up until his death in 1987. Today she continues to study and practice intensively, refining and deepening her understanding of the Buddhist teachings.

Pema Chödrön's writing reaches beyond religious and sectarian boundaries to speak to readers of many faiths and backgrounds. Her popularity as a teacher seems linked to the fact that she does not present herself as an enlightened being but as an ordinary person, writing openly about her own limitations and struggles. Like us, she also gets angry, jealous, and depressed—and precisely because of this she's able to offer guidance that hits home.

I hope you will enjoy these insightful and inspiring selections. In these uncertain times, the teachings presented here can help us to awaken to the fearlessness and clear-seeing that is, as Ani Pema reminds us, our fundamental nature and our greatest resource.

—EDEN STEINBERG
Cambridge, Massachusetts

THE POCKET

PEMA CHÖDRÖN

1

THE NOBLE HEART

Bodhichitta is a Sanskrit word that means "noble or awakened heart." It is said to be present in all beings. Just as butter is inherent in milk and oil is inherent in a sesame seed, this soft spot is inherent in you and me.

It is said that in difficult times, it is only bodhichitta that heals. When inspiration has become hidden, when we feel ready to give up, this is the time when healing can be found in the tenderness of pain itself. This is the time to touch the genuine heart of bodhichitta. In the midst of loneliness, in the midst of fear, in the middle of feeling misunderstood and rejected is the heartbeat of all things, the genuine heart of sadness.

Just as a jewel that has been buried in the earth for a million years is not discolored or harmed, in the same way this noble heart is not affected by all of our kicking and screaming. The jewel can be brought out into the light at any time, and it will glow as brilliantly as if nothing had ever happened. No matter how committed we are to unkindness, selfishness, or greed, the genuine heart of bodhichitta cannot be lost. It is here in all that lives, never marred and completely whole.

2

WE ALREADY HAVE EVERYTHING

We already have everything we need. There is no need for self-improvement. All these trips that we lay on ourselves—the heavy-duty fearing that we're bad and hoping that we're good, the identities that we so dearly cling to, the rage, the jealousy, and the addictions of all kinds—never touch our basic wealth. They are like clouds that temporarily block the sun. But all the time our warmth and brilliance are right here. This is who we really are. We are one blink of an eye away from being fully awake.

Looking at ourselves this way is very different from our usual habit. From this perspective we don't need to change: you can feel as wretched as you like, and you're still a good candidate for enlightenment. You can feel like the world's most hopeless basket case, but that feeling is your wealth, not something to be thrown out or improved upon.

3

THE PATH OF THE BODHISATTVA-WARRIOR

Wherever we are, we can train as a warrior. The practices of meditation, loving-kindness, compassion, joy, and equanimity are our tools. With the help of these practices, we can uncover the soft spot of bodhichitta, the tenderness of the awakened heart. We will find that tenderness in sorrow and in gratitude. We will find it behind the hardness of rage and in the shakiness of fear. It is available in loneliness as well as in kindness.

Many of us prefer practices that will not cause discomfort, yet at the same time we want to be healed. But bodhichitta training doesn't work that way. A warrior accepts that we can never know what will happen to us next. We can try to control the uncontrollable by looking for security and predictability, always hoping to be comfortable and safe. But the truth is that we can never avoid uncertainty. This not knowing is part of the adventure, and it's also what makes us afraid.

Bodhichitta training offers no promise of happy endings. Rather, this "I" who wants to find security—

who wants something to hold on to—can finally learn to grow up. The central question of a warrior's training is not how we avoid uncertainty and fear but how we relate to discomfort. How do we practice with difficulty, with our emotions, with the unpredictable encounters of an ordinary day?

4

RIGHT HERE IS A GOOD PLACE TO START

Start where you are. This is very important. Meditation practice is not about later, when you get it all together and you're this person you really respect. You may be the most violent person in the world—that's a fine place to start. That's a very rich place to start—juicy, smelly. You might be the most depressed person in the world, the most addicted person in the world, the most jealous person in the world. You might think that there are no others on the planet who hate themselves as much as you do. All of that is a good place to start. Just where you are—that's the place to start.

5

LIFE IS A GOOD TEACHER

Life is a good teacher and a good friend. Things are always in transition, if we could only realize it. Nothing ever sums itself up in the way that we like to dream about. The off-center, in-between state is an ideal situation, a situation in which we don't get caught and we can open our hearts and minds beyond limit. It's a very tender, nonaggressive, open-ended state of affairs.

6

WHY MEDITATE?

Why do we meditate? This is a question we'd be wise to ask. Why would we even bother to spend time alone with ourselves?

First of all, it is helpful to understand that meditation is not just about feeling good. To think that this is why we meditate is to set ourselves up for failure. We'll assume we are doing it wrong almost every time we sit down: even the most settled meditator experiences psychological and physical pain. Meditation takes us just as we are, with our confusion and our sanity. This complete acceptance of ourselves as we are is called *maitri*, or unconditional friendliness, a simple, direct relationship with the way we are.

FIND OUT FOR YOURSELF

In all kinds of situations, we can find out what is true simply by studying ourselves in every nook and cranny, in every black hole and bright spot, whether it's murky, creepy, grisly, splendid, spooky, frightening, joyful, inspiring, peaceful, or wrathful. We can just look at the whole thing. There's a lot of encouragement to do this, and meditation gives us the method. When I first encountered Buddhism, I was extremely relieved that there were not only teachings, but also a technique I could use to explore and test these teachings. I was told, from day one, that I had to find out for myself what was true.

8

DIFFICULTY IS INEVITABLE

On a very basic level all beings think that they should be happy. When life becomes difficult or painful, we feel that something has gone wrong. According to the Buddhist teachings, difficulty is inevitable in human life. For one thing, we cannot escape the reality of death. But there are also the realities of aging, of illness, of not getting what we want, and of getting what we don't want. These kinds of difficulties are facts of life. Even if you were the Buddha himself, if you were a fully enlightened person, you would experience death, illness, aging, and sorrow at losing what you love. All of these things would happen to you. If you got burned or cut, it would hurt.

But the Buddhist teachings also say that this is not really what causes us misery in our lives. What causes misery is always trying to get away from the facts of life, always trying to avoid pain and seek happiness—this sense of ours that there could be lasting security and happiness available to us if we could only do the right thing.

It is so basic in us to feel that things should go well

for us, and that if we start to feel depressed, lonely, or inadequate, there's been some kind of mistake or we've lost it. In reality, when you feel depressed, lonely, betrayed, or any unwanted feelings, this is an important moment on the spiritual path. This is when real transformation can take place.

OUR WISDOM IS ALWAYS THERE

The Buddha said that we are never separated from enlightenment. Even at the times we feel most stuck, we are never alienated from the awakened state. This is a revolutionary assertion. Even ordinary people like us with hang-ups and confusion have this mind of enlightenment called *bodhichitta*. The openness and warmth of bodhichitta is in fact our true nature and condition. Even when our neurosis feels far more basic than our wisdom, even when we're feeling most confused and hopeless, bodhichitta—like the open sky—is always here, undiminished by the clouds that temporarily cover it.

10

WE DON'T NEED TO CHANGE OURSELVES

When people start to meditate or to work with any kind of spiritual discipline, they often think that somehow they're going to improve, which is a sort of subtle aggression against who they really are. It's a bit like saying, "If I jog, I'll be a much better person." "If I could only get a nicer house, I'd be a better person." "If I could meditate and calm down, I'd be a better person." Or the scenario may be that they find fault with others; they might say, "If it weren't for my husband, I'd have a perfect marriage." "If it weren't for the fact that my boss and I can't get along, my job would be just great." And "If it weren't for my mind, my meditation would be excellent."

But loving-kindness, or *maitri*, toward ourselves doesn't mean getting rid of anything. Maitri means that we can still be crazy after all these years. We can still be angry after all these years. We can still be timid or jealous or full of feelings of unworthiness. The point is not to try to change ourselves. Meditation practice isn't about trying to throw ourselves away and become something better. It's about befriending who we are already. The ground of practice is you or me or whoever we are right now, just as we are. That's the ground, that's what we study, that's what we come to know with tremendous curiosity and interest.

11

OUR BIRTHRIGHT

When we cling to thoughts and memories, we are clinging to what cannot be grasped. When we touch these phantoms and let them go, we may discover a space, a break in the chatter, a glimpse of open sky. This is our birthright—the wisdom with which we were born, the vast unfolding display of primordial richness, primordial openness, primordial wisdom itself. All that is necessary then is to rest undistract-edly in the immediate present, in this very instant in time. And if we become drawn away by thoughts, by longings, by hopes and fears, again and again we can return to this present moment. We are here. We are carried off as if by the wind, and as if by the wind, we are brought back. When one thought has ended and another has not begun, we can rest in that space. We train in returning to the unchanging heart of this very moment. All compassion and all inspiration come from that.

12

MOVE TOWARD DIFFICULTY

We are told from childhood that something is wrong with us, with the world, and with everything that comes along: it's not perfect, it has rough edges, it has a bitter taste, it's too loud, too soft, too sharp, too wishy-washy. We cultivate a sense of trying to make things better because something is bad here, something is a mistake here, something is a problem here. The main point of the Buddhist teachings is to dissolve the dualistic struggle, our habitual tendency to struggle against what's happening to us or in us. These teachings instruct us to move toward difficulties rather than backing away. We don't get this kind of encouragement very often.

Everything that occurs is not only usable and work-able but is actually the path itself. We can use every-thing that happens to us as the means for waking up. We can use everything that occurs—whether it's our conflicting emotions and thoughts or our seemingly outer situation—to show us where we are asleep and how we can wake up completely, utterly, without res-ervations.

13

FUNDAMENTAL RICHNESS

Fundamental richness is available in each moment. The key is to relax: relax to a cloud in the sky, relax to a tiny bird with gray wings, relax to the sound of the telephone ringing. We can see the simplicity in things as they are. We can smell things, taste things, feel emotions, and have memories. When we are able to be there without saying, "I certainly agree with this," or "I definitely don't agree with that," but just be here very directly, then we find fundamental richness everywhere. It is not ours or theirs but is available always to everyone. In raindrops, in blood drops, in heartache and delight, this wealth is the nature of everything. It is like the sun in that it shines on everyone without discrimination.

14

CULTIVATE LOVING-KINDNESS TOWARD YOURSELF

Some people find the teachings I offer helpful because I encourage them to be kind to themselves. The kindness that I learned from my teachers, and that I wish so much to convey to other people, is kindness toward all qualities of our being. The qualities that are the toughest to be kind to are the painful parts, where we feel ashamed, as if we don't belong, as if we've just blown it, when things are falling apart for us. *Maitri*, or loving-kindness, means sticking with ourselves when we don't have anything, when we feel like a loser. And it becomes the basis for extending the same unconditional friendliness with others.

15

A MORE ADVENTUROUS
WAY TO LIVE

There's a common misunderstanding among all the human beings who have ever been born on the earth that the best way to live is to try to avoid pain and just try to get comfortable. You can see this even in insects and animals and birds. All of us are the same.

A much more interesting, kind, adventurous, and joyful approach to life is to begin to develop our curiosity, not caring whether the object of our inquisitiveness is bitter or sweet. To lead a life that goes beyond pettiness and prejudice and always wanting to make sure that everything turns out on our own terms, to lead a more passionate, full, and delightful life than that, we must realize that we can endure a lot of pain and pleasure for the sake of finding out who we are and what this world is, how we tick and how our world ticks, how the whole thing just *is*.

16

WHEN YOU OPEN UP
TO LIFE AS IT IS

When you open yourself to the continually changing, impermanent, dynamic nature of your own being
and of reality, you increase your capacity to love and
care about other people and your capacity to not be
afraid. You're able to keep your eyes open, your heart
open, and your mind open. And you notice when you
get caught up in prejudice, bias, and aggression. You
develop an enthusiasm for no longer watering those
negative seeds, from now until the day you die. And
you begin to think of your life as offering endless op-
portunities to start to do things differently.

17

DON'T LET LIFE HARDEN
YOUR HEART

When I was about six years old, I received an essential teaching from an old woman sitting in the sun. I was walking by her house one day feeling lonely, unloved, and mad, kicking anything I could find. Laughing, she said to me, "Little girl, don't you go letting life harden your heart."

Right there, I received this pith instruction: we can let the circumstances of our lives harden us so that we become increasingly resentful and afraid, or we can let them soften us and make us kinder and more open to what scares us. We always have this choice.

18

OUR HUMAN SITUATION
(THE THREE MARKS
OF EXISTENCE)

The Buddha taught that there are three principal characteristics of human existence: impermanence, egolessness, and suffering (or dissatisfaction). The lives of all beings are marked by these three qualities. Recognizing these qualities to be real and true in our own experience helps us to relax with things as they are.

I feel gratitude to the Buddha for pointing out that what we struggle against all our lives can be acknowledged as ordinary experience. Life *does* continually go up and down. People and situations *are* unpredictable and so is everything else. Everybody knows the pain of getting what we don't want: saints, sinners, winners, losers. I feel gratitude that someone saw the truth and pointed out that we don't suffer this kind of pain because of our personal inability to get things right.

When I begin to doubt that I have what it takes to stay present with impermanence, egolessness, and suffering, it uplifts me to remember that there is no cure for the facts of life. This teaching on the three marks of existence can motivate us to stop struggling against the nature of reality. We can stop harming others and ourselves in our efforts to escape the alternation of pleasure and pain. We can relax and be fully present for our lives.

UNCONDITIONAL WELL-BEING

When you begin to touch your heart or let your heart be touched, you begin to discover that it's bottomless, that it doesn't have any resolution, that this heart is huge, vast, and limitless. You begin to discover how much warmth and gentleness is there, as well as how much space. Your world seems less solid, more roomy and spacious. The burden lightens. In the beginning it might feel like sadness or a shaky feeling, accompanied by a lot of fear, but your willingness to feel the fear, to make fear your companion, is growing. You're willing to get to know yourself at this deep level. After a while this same feeling begins to turn into a longing to be fully human and to live in your world without always having to shut down and close off when certain things come along. It begins to turn into a longing to be there for your friends when they're in trouble, to be of real help to this poor, aching planet. Curiously enough, along with this longing and this sadness and this tenderness, there's an immense sense of well-being, unconditional well-being, which doesn't have anything to do with pleasant or unpleasant, good or bad, hope or fear, disgrace or fame. It's something that simply comes to you when you feel that you can keep your heart open.

20

DEVELOPING TRUE COURAGE

As long as we're caught up in always looking for certainty and happiness, rather than honoring the taste and smell and quality of exactly what is happening, as long as we're always running away from discomfort, we're going to be caught in a cycle of unhappiness and disappointment, and we will feel weaker and weaker.

Instead of asking ourselves, "How can I find security and happiness?" we could ask ourselves, "Can I touch the center of my pain? Can I sit with suffering, both yours and mine, without trying to make it go away? Can I stay present to the ache of loss or disgrace—disappointment in all its many forms—and let it open me?" This is the trick.

21

NOTHING IS FIXED

As human beings we are as impermanent as everything else is. Every cell in the body is continuously changing. Thoughts and emotions rise and fall away unceasingly. When we're thinking that we're competent or that we're hopeless—what are we basing it on? On this fleeting moment? On yesterday's success or failure? We cling to a fixed idea of who we are and it cripples us. Nothing and no one is fixed.

22

GETTING THE KNACK
OF HOPELESSNESS

Turning your mind toward the dharma does not bring
security or confirmation. Turning your mind toward
the dharma does not bring any ground to stand on. In
fact, when your mind turns toward the dharma, you
fearlessly acknowledge impermanence and change and
begin to get the knack of hopelessness.

In Tibetan there's an interesting word: *ye tang
che*. The *ye* part means "totally, completely," and the
rest of it means "exhausted." Altogether, *ye tang che*
means totally tired out. We might say "totally fed up."
It describes an experience of complete hopelessness,
of completely giving up hope. This is an important
point. This is the beginning of the beginning. Without
giving up hope—that there's somewhere better to be,
that there's someone better to be—we will never relax with where we are or who we are.

To think that we can finally get it all together is un-
realistic. To seek for some lasting security is futile. To
undo our very ancient and very stuck habitual patterns
of mind requires that we begin to turn around some of

our most basic assumptions. Believing in a solid, separate self, continuing to seek pleasure and avoid pain, thinking that someone "out there" is to blame for our pain—one has to get totally fed up with these ways of thinking. One has to give up hope that this way of thinking will bring us satisfaction. Suffering begins to dissolve when we can question the belief or the hope that there's anywhere to hide.

23

THIS BRIEF LIFETIME

How are we going to spend this brief lifetime? Are we going to strengthen our well-perfected ability to struggle against uncertainty, or are we going to train in letting go? Are we going to hold on stubbornly to "I'm like this and you're like that"? Or are we going to move beyond that narrow mind? Could we start to train as a warrior, aspiring to reconnect with the natural flexibility of our being and to help others do the same? If we start to move in this direction, limitless possibilities will begin to open up.

24

DISSOLVING OUR
SELF-IMPORTANCE

The fixed idea that we have about ourselves as solid and separate from each other is painfully limiting. It is possible to move through the drama of our lives without believing so earnestly in the character that we play. That we take ourselves so seriously, that we are so absurdly important in our own minds, is a problem for us. We feel justified in being annoyed with everything. We feel justified in denigrating ourselves or in feeling that we are more clever than other people. Self-importance hurts us, limiting us to the narrow world of our likes and dislikes. We end up bored to death with ourselves and our world. We end up never satisfied.

We have two alternatives: either we question our beliefs—or we don't. Either we accept our fixed versions of reality—or we begin to challenge them. In Buddha's opinion, to train in staying open and curious—to train in dissolving our assumptions and beliefs—is the best use of our human lives.

25

RECOGNIZING OUR
KINSHIP WITH OTHERS

Our personal attempts to live humanely in this world are never wasted. Choosing to cultivate love rather than anger just might be what it takes to save the planet from extinction.

What is it that allows our goodwill to expand and our prejudice and anger to decrease? This is a significant question. Traditionally it is said that the root of aggression and suffering is ignorance. But what is it that we are ignoring? Entrenched in the tunnel vision of our personal concerns, what we ignore is our kinship with others. One reason we train as warrior-bodhisattvas is to recognize our interconnectedness—to grow in understanding that when we harm another, we are harming ourselves. So we train in recognizing our uptightness. We train in seeing that others are not so different from ourselves. We train in opening our hearts and minds in increasingly difficult situations.

26

DISCOVER THE GENUINE HEART OF SADNESS

Bodhichitta is our heart—our wounded, softened heart. Now, if you look for that soft heart that we guard so carefully—if you decide that you're going to do a scientific exploration under the microscope and try to find that heart—you won't find it. You can look, but all you'll find is some kind of tenderness. There isn't anything that you can cut out and put under the microscope. There isn't anything that you can dissect or grasp. The more you look, the more you find just a feeling of tenderness tinged with some kind of sadness. This sadness is not about somebody mistreating us. This is inherent sadness, unconditioned sadness. It is part of our birthright, a family heirloom. It's been called the genuine heart of sadness.

27

WE START WITH OURSELVES

In cultivating loving-kindness, we train first to be honest, loving, and compassionate toward ourselves. Rather than nurturing self-denigration, we begin to cultivate a clear-seeing kindness. Sometimes we feel good and strong. Sometimes we feel inadequate and weak. But our loving-kindness is unconditional. No matter how we feel, we can aspire to be happy. We can learn to act and think in ways that sow seeds of our future well-being, gradually becoming more aware of what causes happiness as well as what causes distress. Without loving-kindness for ourselves it is difficult, if not impossible, to genuinely feel it for others.

HAPPINESS WITHOUT
A HANGOVER

As we train in opening our hearts and discovering the soft spot, we gradually feel more joy, the joy that comes from a growing appreciation of our basic goodness. We still experience strong conflicting emotions, we still experience the illusion of separateness, but there's a fundamental openness that we begin to trust. This trust in our fresh, unbiased nature brings us unlimited joy—a happiness that's completely devoid of clinging and craving. This is the joy of happiness without a hangover.

How do we cultivate the conditions for joy to expand? We train in staying present. In sitting meditation, we train in mindfulness and unconditional friendliness: in being steadfast with our bodies, our emotions, our thoughts. We stay with our own little plot of earth and trust that it can be cultivated, that cultivation will bring it to its full potential. Even though it's full of rocks and the soil is dry, we begin to plow this plot with patience. We let the process evolve naturally.

At the beginning joy is just a feeling that our own situation is workable. We stop looking for a more suitable place to be. We've discovered that the continual search for something better does not work out. This doesn't mean that there are suddenly flowers growing where before there were only rocks. It means we have confidence that something will grow here. As we cultivate our garden, the conditions become more conducive to the growth of bodhichitta. The joy comes from not giving up on ourselves, from mindfully sticking with ourselves and beginning to experience our great warrior spirit.

29

REJOICE IN ORDINARY LIFE

We can learn to rejoice in even the smallest blessings our life holds. It is easy to miss our own good fortune; often happiness comes in ways we don't even notice. It's like a cartoon I saw of an astonished-looking man saying, "What was that?" The caption below read, "Bob experiences a moment of well-being." The ordinariness of our good fortune can make it hard to catch.

The key is to be here, fully connected with the moment, paying attention to the details of ordinary life. By taking care of ordinary things—our pots and pans, our clothing, our teeth—we rejoice in them. When we scrub a vegetable or brush our hair, we are expressing appreciation: friendship toward ourselves and toward the living quality that is found in everything. This combination of mindfulness and appreciation connects us fully with reality and brings us joy.

30

OVERCOMING UNWORTHINESS

Remind yourself, in whatever way is personally mean-ingful, that it is not in your best interest to reinforce thoughts and feelings of unworthiness. Even if you've already taken the bait and feel the familiar pull of self-denigration, marshal your intelligence, courage, and humor in order to turn the tide. Ask yourself: Do I want to strengthen what I'm feeling now? Do I want to cut myself off from my basic goodness? Remind yourself that your fundamental nature is unconditionally open and free.

31

BEYOND RIGHT AND WRONG

Compassionate action, being there for others, being able to act and speak in a way that communicates, starts with seeing ourselves when we start to make ourselves right or make ourselves wrong. At that particular point, we could just contemplate the fact that there is a larger alternative to either of those, a more tender, shaky kind of place where we could live. This place, if we can touch it, will help us train ourselves throughout our lives to open further to whatever we feel, to open further rather than shut down more. We'll find that as we begin to commit ourselves to this practice, as we begin to have a sense of celebrating the aspects of ourselves that we found so impossible before, something will shift in us. Something will shift permanently in us. Our ancient habitual patterns will begin to soften, and we'll begin to see the faces and hear the words of people who are talking to us.

OVERCOMING SELF-DECEPTION

The essence of bravery is being without self-deception. However it's not so easy to take a straight look at what we do. Seeing ourselves clearly is initially uncomfortable and embarrassing. As we train in clarity and steadfastness, we see things we'd prefer to deny—judgmentalness, pettiness, arrogance. These are not sins but temporary and workable habits of mind. The more we get to know them, the more they lose their power. This is how we come to trust that our basic nature is utterly simple, free of struggle between good and bad.

33

INTO THE DEMON'S MOUTH

Milarepa, who lived in the eleventh century, is one of the heroes of Tibetan Buddhism, one of the brave ones. He was also a rather unusual fellow. He was a loner who lived in caves by himself and meditated wholeheartedly for years. He was extremely stubborn and determined. If he couldn't find anything to eat for a couple of years, he just ate nettles and turned green, but he would never stop practicing.

The story goes that one evening Milarepa returned to his cave after gathering firewood, only to find it filled with demons. They were cooking his food, reading his books, sleeping in his bed. They had taken over the joint. He knew about the teaching of the nonduality of self and other, but he still didn't quite know how to get these guys out of his cave. Even though he had the sense that they were just a projection of his own mind—all the unwanted parts of himself—he didn't know how to get rid of them.

So first he taught them the dharma. He sat on this seat that was higher than they were and said things to them about how we are all one. He talked about compassion and emptiness and other key Buddhist teachings. Nothing happened. The demons were still there. Then he lost his patience and got angry and ran at them. They just laughed at him. Finally, he gave up and just sat down on the floor, saying, "I'm not going away and it looks like you're not either, so let's just live here together."

At that point, all of them left except one. Milarepa said, "This one is particularly vicious." (We all know that one. Sometimes we have lots of them like that. Sometimes we feel that's all we've got.) He didn't know what to do, so he surrendered himself even further. He walked over and put himself right into the mouth of the demon and said, "Just eat me up if you want to." Then that demon left too. The moral of the story is, when the resistance is gone, so are the demons.

EDGING TOWARD THE OPEN STATE

We might assume that as we train in bodhichitta, our habitual patterns will start to unwind—that day by day, month by month, we'll be more open-minded, more flexible, more of a warrior. But what actually happens with ongoing practice is that our patterns intensify. In vajrayana Buddhism this is called "heightened neurosis." It's not something we do on purpose. It just happens. We catch the scent of groundlessness, and despite our wishes to remain steady, open, and flexible, we hold on tight in very habitual ways.

This has been the experience of everyone who ever set out on the path of awakening. All those smiling enlightened people you see in pictures or in person had to go through the process of encountering their full-blown neurosis, their methods of looking for ground. When we start to interrupt our ordinary ways of calling ourselves names and patting ourselves on the back, we are doing something extremely brave. Slowly we edge toward the open state, but let's face it, we are moving toward a place of no handholds, no footholds, no mindholds.

HAVE NO EXPECTATIONS, JUST BE KIND

A meditation student I was working with, whom I'll call Dan, had a serious alcohol and drug problem. He was really making great strides, and then he went on a binge. On the day I found out about it I happened to have an opportunity to see my teacher Trungpa Rinpoche. I blurted out to him how upset I was that Dan had gone on a binge. I was so disappointed. Rinpoche got really angry; it completely stopped my heart and mind. He said that being upset about Dan's binge was my problem. "You should never have expectations for other people. Just be kind to them," he told me. In terms of Dan, I should just help him keep walking forward inch by inch and be kind to him— invite him for dinner, give him little gifts, and do anything to bring some happiness to his life—instead of having these big goals for him. He said that setting goals for others can be aggressive—really wanting a success story for ourselves. When we do this to others, we are asking them to live up to our ideals. Instead, we should just be kind.

36

DIFFICULT PEOPLE HELP US TO LEARN AND GROW

Gurdjieff was a renowned spiritual teacher who lived in the early part of the twentieth century. There was a man in his community who was really bad tempered. Nobody could stand this guy because he was so prickly. Every little thing caused him to spin off into a tantrum. Everything irritated him. He complained constantly, so everyone felt the need to tiptoe around him because anything that might be said could cause him to explode. People just wished that he would go away.

Gurdjieff liked to make his students do things that were completely meaningless. One day there were about forty people out cutting up a lawn into little pieces and moving it to another place on the grounds. This was too much for this fellow; it was the last straw. He blew up, stormed out, got in his car, and drove off, whereupon there was a spontaneous celebration. People were thrilled, so happy he had gone. But when they told Gurdjieff what had happened, he said, "Oh no!" and went after him in his car.

Three days later they both came back. That night when Gurdjieff's attendant was serving him his supper, he asked, "Sir, why did you bring him back?" Gurdjieff answered in a very low voice, "You're not going to believe this, and this is just between you and me; you must tell no one. I pay him to stay here."

37

AT THE BEGINNING
AND AT THE END

In the morning when you wake up, reflect on the day ahead and aspire to use it to keep a wide-open heart and mind. At the end of the day, before going to sleep, think over what you've done. If you fulfilled your aspiration, even once, rejoice in that. If you went against your aspiration, rejoice that you are able to see what you did and are no longer living in ignorance. This way you will be inspired to go forward with increasing clarity, confidence, and compassion.

38

NO HAPPY ENDING

In one of the first teachings I ever heard, the teacher said, "I don't know why you came here, but I want to tell you right now that the basis of this whole teaching is that you're never going to get it all together." I felt a little like he had just slapped me in the face or thrown cold water over my head, but I've always remembered it. There isn't going to be some precious future time when all the loose ends will be tied up. Even though it was shocking to me, it rang true. One of the things that keeps us unhappy is this continual searching for pleasure or security, searching for a little more comfortable situation, either at the domestic level or at the spiritual level or at the level of mental peace.

39

SHARING THE HEART

Sharing the heart is a simple practice that can be used at any time and in every situation. It enlarges our view and helps us remember our interconnection. The essence of this practice is that when we encounter pain in our life we breathe into our heart with the recognition that others also feel this. It's a way of acknowledging when we are closing down and of training to open up. When we encounter any pleasure or tenderness in our life, we cherish that and rejoice. Then we make the wish that others could also experience this delight or this relief. In a nutshell, when life is pleasant, think of others. When life is a burden, think of others. If this is the only training we ever remember to do, it will benefit us tremendously and everyone else as well. It's a way of bringing whatever we encounter onto the path of awakening bodhichitta.

40

EMBRACING OUR DIFFERENCES

We *are* different; we are very different from each
other. One person's idea of what is polite is someone
else's idea of what is rude. In some cultures it's con-
sidered rude to belch when you're eating, and in others it shows that you enjoyed your meal. What might
smell repulsive to one person might smell wonderful
to another. We are really different, and we have to
acknowledge that. But instead of going to war because
of our differences, let's play soccer. It will be a strange
game, given our instruction to let others have the victory and keep the defeat to ourselves, but that doesn't
mean that we play to lose; it means that we play to
play. We could play *together*, even though we're on
opposite teams. There are no big stakes, just playing.
There are different teams; otherwise the game won't
work. But it doesn't have to lead to World War III or
the destruction of the planet.

41

BEING THERE FOR OTHERS

To relate with others compassionately is a challenge. Really communicating from the heart and being there for someone else—our child, spouse, parent, client, patient, or the homeless woman on the street—means not shutting down on that person, which means, first of all, not shutting down on ourselves. This means allowing ourselves to feel what we feel and not pushing it away. It means accepting every aspect of ourselves, even the parts we don't like. To do this requires openness, which in Buddhism is sometimes called emptiness—not fixating or holding on to anything.

42

BEING BIG AND SMALL
AT THE SAME TIME

I was once invited to teach with the Sakyong Mipham Rinpoche, my teacher's eldest son, in a situation where it wasn't exactly clear what my status was. Sometimes I was treated as a big deal who should come in through a special door and sit in a special seat. Then I'd think, "Okay, I'm a big deal." I'd start running with that idea and come up with big-deal notions about how things should be.

Then I'd get the message, "Oh, no, no, no. You should just sit on the floor and mix with everybody and be one of the crowd." Okay. So now the message was that I should just be ordinary, not set myself up or be the teacher. But as soon as I was getting comfortable with being humble, I would be asked to do something special that only big deals did.

This was a painful experience because I was always being insulted and humiliated by my own expectations. As soon as I was sure how it should be, so I could feel secure, I would get a message that it should be the other way. Finally I said to the Sakyong, "This is really hurting. I just don't know who I'm supposed to be," and he said, "Well, you have to learn to be big and small at the same time."

43

WHEN ANGER ARISES, REMEMBER TO PAUSE

When you feel like a keg of dynamite just about to go off, patience means just slowing down at that point—just pausing—instead of immediately acting on your usual, habitual response. You refrain from acting, stop talking to yourself, and connect with the soft spot. But at the same time you are completely and totally honest with yourself about what you are feeling. You're not suppressing anything; patience has nothing to do with suppression. In fact, it has everything to do with a gentle, honest relationship with yourself.

If you wait and don't fuel the rage with your thoughts, you can be very honest about the fact that you long for revenge; nevertheless you keep interrupting the torturous story line and stay with the underlying vulnerability. That frustration, that uneasiness and vulnerability is nothing solid. And yet it is painful to experience. Still, just wait and be patient with your anguish and with the discomfort of it. This means relaxing with that restless, hot energy—knowing that it's the only way to find peace for ourselves or the world.

44

GLORIOUSNESS AND WRETCHEDNESS

Life is glorious, but life is also wretched. It is both. Appreciating the gloriousness inspires us, encourages us, cheers us up, gives us a bigger perspective, energizes us. We feel connected. But if that's all that's happening, we get arrogant and start to look down on others, and there is a sense of making ourselves a big deal and being really serious about it, wanting it to be like that forever. The gloriousness becomes tinged by craving and addiction.

On the other hand, wretchedness—life's painful aspect—softens us up considerably. Knowing pain is a very important ingredient of being there for another person. When you are feeling a lot of grief, you can look right into somebody's eyes because you feel you haven't got anything to lose—you're just there. The wretchedness humbles us and softens us, but if we were only wretched, we would all just go down the tubes. We'd be so depressed, discouraged, and hopeless that we wouldn't have enough energy to eat an apple. Gloriousness and wretchedness need each other. One inspires us, the other softens us. They go together.

45

THE PERFECTION OF PATIENCE

Patience is not learned in safety. It is not learned when everything is harmonious and going well. When everything is smooth sailing, who needs patience? If you stay in your room with the door locked and the curtains drawn, everything may seem harmonious, but the minute anything doesn't go your way, you blow up. There is no cultivation of patience when your pattern is to just try to seek harmony and smooth everything out. Patience implies willingness to be alive rather than trying to seek harmony.

A hermit well known for his austerity had been meditating in a cave for twenty years. An unconventional teacher named Patrul Rinpoche showed up at the cave, and the hermit humbly and sweetly welcomed him in. Patrul Rinpoche said, "Tell me, what have you been doing here?" "I've been practicing the perfection of patience," the hermit answered.

Putting his face very close to the hermit's face, Patrul Rinpoche said, "But a pair of old scoundrels like us, we don't care anything about patience really. We only do this to get everyone's admiration, right? We just do this to get people to think we are big shots, don't we?"

And the hermit started getting irritated. But Patrul Rinpoche wouldn't stop. He just kept laughing and patting him on the back and saying, "Yeah, we sure know how to dupe people, don't we? We really know. I'll bet they bring you a lot of gifts, don't they?"

At this point the hermit stood up and screamed, "Why did you come here? Why are you tormenting me? Go away and leave me in peace!" And then the Rinpoche said, "So now, where is your perfection of patience?"

So that's the point. We can create the ideal situation in which we have a very high opinion of ourselves, but how do we do when it comes to the big squeeze, the collision of our vision with the reality of the situation?

HOW TO DEFEAT FEAR

Once there was a young warrior. Her teacher told her that she had to do battle with fear. She didn't want to do that. It seemed too aggressive; it was scary; it seemed unfriendly. But the teacher said she had to do it and gave her the instructions for the battle. The day arrived. The student warrior stood on one side, and fear stood on the other. The warrior was feeling very small, and fear was looking big and wrathful. They both had their weapons. The young warrior roused herself and went toward fear, prostrated three times, and asked, "May I have permission to go into battle with you?" Fear said, "Thank you for showing me so much respect that you ask permission." Then the young warrior said, "How can I defeat you?" Fear replied, "My weapons are that I talk fast, and I get very close to your face. Then you get completely unnerved, and you do whatever I say. If you don't do what I tell you, I have no power. You can listen to me, and you can have respect for me. You can even be convinced by me. But if you don't do what I say, I have no power." In that way, the student warrior learned how to defeat fear.

47

WE HAVE MET THE ENEMY— AND THE FRIEND

It was Pogo, a cartoon character created by Walt Kelly, who said, "We have met the enemy and he is us." This particular slogan now appears a lot in the environmental movement. It isn't somebody else who's polluting the rivers —it's us. The cause of confusion and bewilderment and pollution and violence isn't really someone else's problem: it's something we can come to know in ourselves. But in order to do that we have to understand that *we have met the friend and he is me*. The more we make friends with ourselves, the more we can see that our ways of shutting down and closing off are rooted in the mistaken thinking that the way to get happy is to blame somebody else.

It's a little uncertain who is "us" and who is "them." Bernard Glassman Roshi, who does a lot of work with the homeless in New York, said that he doesn't work with the homeless because he's such a great guy but because going into the areas of society that he has rejected is the only way to make friends with the parts of himself that he's rejected. It's all interrelated. *We work on ourselves in order to help others, but also we help others in order to work on ourselves.* That's a very important point.

48

CONNECT WITH
UNCONDITIONAL OPENNESS

When we sit down to meditate, we can connect with something unconditional—a state of mind, a basic environment that does not grasp or reject anything. Meditation is probably the only activity that doesn't add anything to the picture. Everything is allowed to come and go without further embellishment. Meditation is a totally nonviolent, nonaggressive occupation. Not filling the space, allowing for the possibility of connecting with unconditional openness—this provides the basis for real change.

49

THE DARING OF HAVING
NO ENEMIES

Whether it's ourselves, our lovers, bosses, children, a local Scrooge, or the political situation, it's more daring and real not to shut anyone out of our hearts and not to make the other into an enemy. If we begin to live like this, we'll find that we actually can't make things completely right or completely wrong anymore, because things are a lot more slippery and playful than that. Everything is ambiguous; everything is always shifting and changing, and there are as many different takes on any given situation as there are people involved. Trying to find absolute rights and wrongs is a trick we play on ourselves to feel secure and comfortable.

MIRROR, MIRROR ON THE WALL

If we are wholehearted about wanting to be there for other people without shutting anybody or anything out of our hearts, our pretty little self-image of how kind or compassionate we are gets completely blown. We're always being tested and we're always meeting our match. The more you're willing to open your heart, the more challenges come along that make you want to shut it.

You can't do this work in a safety zone. You have to go out into the marketplace and live your life like everybody else, but with the added ingredient of not wanting to shut anything out of your heart. Maitri— loving-kindness—has to go very deep, because when you practice it, you're going to see everything about yourself. Every time your buttons get pushed is like a big mirror showing you your own face, and like the evil stepmother in *Snow White and the Seven Dwarfs*, you want the mirror to tell you what you want to hear— even if it's that you haven't been kind or that you're selfish. Somehow you can even use your insight into your limitations to keep yourself feeling all right.

What we don't want is any *unforeseen* feedback from the mirror. What we don't want is to be naked, exposed. We have blind spots, and we put a lot of energy into staying blind. One day the wicked stepmother went to the mirror and said, "Mirror, mirror, on the wall, who's the fairest of them all?" and instead of, "You are, sweetheart," the mirror said, "Snow White." And just like us, she didn't want to hear it. Nevertheless, I think we all know that there's no point in blaming the mirror when it shows you your own face, and there's certainly no point in breaking the mirror.

51

EVERYTHING HAS TO GO

All of us are like eagles who have forgotten that we know how to fly. The teachings are reminding us who we are and what we can do. They help us notice that we're in a nest with a lot of old food, excrement, and stale air. From when we were very young we've had this longing to see those mountains in the distance and experience that big sky and the vast ocean, but somehow we got trapped in our nest, just because we forgot that we knew how to fly. We are like eagles, but we have on underwear and pants and shirt and socks and shoes and a hat and coat and boots and mittens and an iPod and dark glasses, and it occurs to us that we could experience that vast sky, but we'd better start taking off some of this stuff. So we take off the coat and the hat and it's cold, but we know that we have to do it, and we teeter on the edge of the nest and we take off. Then we find out for ourselves that everything has to go. You just can't fly when you are wearing socks and shoes and coats and pants and underwear. Everything has to go.

THE JOURNEY GOES DOWN, NOT UP

Spiritual awakening is frequently described as a journey to the top of a mountain. We leave our attachments and our worldliness behind and slowly make our way to the top. At the peak we have transcended all pain. The only problem with this metaphor is that we leave all the others behind—our drunken brother, our schizophrenic sister, our tormented animals and friends. Their suffering continues, unrelieved by our personal escape.

In the process of discovering bodhichitta, the journey goes down, not up. It's as if the mountain pointed toward the center of the earth instead of reaching into the sky. Instead of transcending the suffering of all creatures, we move toward the turbulence and doubt. We jump into it. We slide into it. We tiptoe into it. We move toward it however we can. We explore the reality and unpredictability of insecurity and pain, and we try not to push it away. If it takes years, if it takes lifetimes, we let it be as it is. At our own pace, without speed or aggression, we move down and down and down. With us move millions of others, our companions in awakening from fear. At the bottom we discover water, the healing water of bodhichitta. Right down there in the thick of things, we discover the love that will not die.

53

WHEN THINGS FALL APART

Things falling apart is a kind of testing and also a kind of healing. We think that the point is to pass the test or to overcome the problem, but the truth is that things don't really get solved. They come together and they fall apart. Then they come together again and fall apart again. It's just like that. The healing comes from letting there be room for all of this to happen: room for grief, for relief, for misery, for joy.

54

BEING GENTLE WITH OURSELVES

Gentleness in our practice and in our life helps to awaken the genuine heart of bodhichitta. It's like remembering something. This compassion, this clarity, this openness is like something we have forgotten. Sitting here being gentle with ourselves, we're rediscovering something. It's like a mother reuniting with her child; having been lost to each other for a long, long time, they reunite. The way to reunite with the genuine heart of bodhichitta is to lighten up in your practice and in your whole life.

55

WE NEVER KNOW

When we think that something is going to bring us pleasure, we don't know what's really going to happen. When we think something is going to give us misery, we don't know. Letting there be room for not knowing is the most important thing of all. We try to do what we think is going to help. But we don't know. We never know if we're going to fall flat or sit up tall. When there's a big disappointment, we don't know if that's the end of the story. It may be just the beginning of a great adventure.

I read somewhere about a family who had only one son. They were very poor. This son was extremely precious to them, and the only thing that mattered to his family was that he bring them some financial support and prestige. Then he was thrown from a horse and crippled. It seemed like the end of their lives. Two weeks after that, the army came into the village and took away all the healthy, strong men to fight in the war, and this young man was allowed to stay behind and take care of his family.

Life is like that. We don't know anything. We call something bad; we call it good. But really we just don't know.

OPENING THE DOOR TO LIFE

Pain is a result of what's called ego clinging, of wanting things to work out on our own terms, of wanting "me-victorious."

Ego is like a room of your own, a room with a view, with the temperature and the smells and the music that you like. You want it your own way. You'd just like to have a little peace; you'd like to have a little happiness, you know, just "gimme a break!"

But the more you think that way, the more you try to get life to come out so that it will always suit you, the more your fear of other people and what's outside your room grows. Rather than becoming more relaxed, you start pulling down the shades and locking the door. When you do go out, you find the experience more and more unsettling and disagreeable. You become touchier, more fearful, more irritable than ever. The more you just try to get it your way, the less you feel at home.

To begin to develop compassion for yourself and others, you have to unlock the door. You don't open it yet, because you have to work with your fear that somebody you don't like might come in. Then as you begin to relax and befriend those feelings, you begin to open it. Sure enough, in come the music and the smells that you don't like. Sure enough, someone puts a foot in and tells you you should be a different religion or vote for someone you don't like or give money that you don't want to give.

Now you begin to relate with those feelings. You develop some compassion, connecting with the soft spot. You relate with what begins to happen when you're not protecting yourself so much. Then gradually, you become more curious than afraid. To be fearless isn't really to overcome fear, it's to come to know its nature. Just open the door more and more and at some point you'll feel capable of inviting all sentient beings as your guests.

SEEK LONG-TERM RELIEF

We act out because, ironically, we think it will bring us some relief. We equate it with happiness. Often there *is* some relief, for the moment. When you have an addiction and you fulfill that addiction, there is a moment in which you feel some relief. Then the nightmare gets worse. So it is with aggression. When you get to tell someone off, you might feel pretty good for a while, but somehow the sense of righteous indignation and hatred grows, and it hurts you. It's as if you pick up hot coals with your bare hands and throw them at your enemy. If the coals happen to hit him, he will be hurt. But in the meantime, you are guaranteed to be burned.

On the other hand, if we begin to surrender to ourselves—begin to drop the story line and experience what all this messy stuff behind the story line feels like—we begin to find bodhichitta, the tenderness that's under all that harshness. By being kind to ourselves, we become kind to others. By being kind to others—if it's done properly, with proper understanding—we benefit as well.

58

AM I GOING TO ADD TO
THE AGGRESSION?

Every day we could think about the aggression in
the world, in New York, Los Angeles, Darfur, Iraq,
everywhere. All over the world, everybody always
strikes out at the enemy, and the pain escalates forever. Every day we could reflect on this and ask ourselves, "Am I going to add to the aggression in the
world?" Every day, at the moment when things get
edgy, we can just ask ourselves, "Am I going to practice peace, or am I going to war?"

59

WAKEFULNESS IS FOUND
IN PLEASURE AND PAIN

In practicing meditation, we're not trying to live up to some kind of ideal—quite the opposite. We're just being with our experience, whatever it is. If our experience is that sometimes we have some kind of perspective, and sometimes we have none, then that's our experience. If sometimes we can approach what scares us, and sometimes we absolutely can't, then that's our experience. "This very moment is the perfect teacher, and it's always with us" is really a most profound instruction. Just seeing what's going on—that's the teaching right there. We can be with what's happening and not dissociate. Awakeness is found in our pleasure and our pain, our confusion and our wisdom, available in each moment of our weird, unfathomable, ordinary everyday lives.

60

BE GRATEFUL TO EVERYONE

Others will always show you exactly where you are stuck. They say or do something and you automatically get hooked into a familiar way of reacting—shutting down, speeding up, or getting all worked up. When you react in the habitual way, with anger, greed, and so forth, it gives you a chance to see your patterns and work with them honestly and compassionately. Without others provoking you, you remain ignorant of your painful habits and cannot train in transforming them into the path of awakening.

61

THERE IS NO CURE
FOR HOT AND COLD

The way to dissolve our resistance to life is to meet it face-to-face. When we feel resentment because the room is too hot, we could meet the heat and feel its fieriness and its heaviness. When we feel resentment because the room is too cold, we could meet the cold and feel its iciness and its bite. When we want to complain about the rain, we could feel its wetness instead. When we worry because the wind is shaking our windows, we could meet the wind and hear its sound. Cutting our expectations for a cure is a gift we can give ourselves. There is no cure for hot and cold. They will go on forever. After we have died, the ebb and flow will still continue. Like the tides of the sea, like day and night—this is the nature of things. Being able to appreciate, being able to look closely, being able to open our minds—this is the core of maitri.

62

LOOK FOR THE GAPS

In my own training, I've been taught to look for the gaps: the gap at the end of each out-breath; the space between thoughts; the naturally occurring, nonconceptual pause after a sudden shock, unexpected noise, or moment of awe. Trungpa Rinpoche advised intentionally creating these gaps by pausing to look at the sky or stopping to listen intently. He called this "poking holes in the clouds."

These fleeting moments of no-big-deal me, no internal conversations, no frozen opinions, are very simple yet powerful. The utter freshness of just being present introduces us to unshakable confidence: a lionlike pride that refuses to buy into any negative or limiting story lines.

DON'T CAUSE HARM

Not causing harm obviously includes not killing or robbing or lying to people. It also includes not being aggressive—not being aggressive with our actions, our speech, or our minds. Learning not to cause harm to ourselves or others is a basic Buddhist teaching on the healing power of nonaggression.

Not harming ourselves or others in the beginning, not harming ourselves or others in the middle, and not harming ourselves or others in the end is the basis of enlightened society. This is how there could be a sane world. It starts with sane citizens, and that is us. The most fundamental aggression to ourselves, the most fundamental harm we can do to ourselves, is to remain ignorant by not having the courage and the respect to look at ourselves honestly and gently.

64

LONELINESS

Usually we regard loneliness as an enemy. Heartache is not something we choose to invite in. It's restless and pregnant and hot with the desire to escape and find something or someone to keep us company. When we can rest in the middle, we begin to have a nonthreatening relationship with loneliness, a relaxing and cooling loneliness that completely turns our usual fearful patterns upside down.

65

LET THE THINGS THAT ENTER YOUR LIFE WAKE YOU UP

Life's work is to wake up, to let the things that enter into your life wake you up rather than put you to sleep. The only way to do this is to open, be curious, and develop some sense of sympathy for everything that comes along, to get to know its nature and let it teach you what it will. It's going to stick around until you learn your lesson, at any rate. You can leave your marriage, you can quit your job, you can only go where people are going to praise you, you can manipulate your world until you're blue in the face to try to make it always smooth, but the same old demons will always come up until finally you have learned your lesson, the lesson they came to teach you. Then those same demons will appear as friendly, warmhearted companions on the path.

TRAIN IN THE MIDDLE WAY

The middle way is wide open, but it's tough going, because it goes against the grain of an ancient neurotic pattern that we all share. When we feel lonely, when we feel hopeless, what we want to do is move to the right or the left. We don't want to sit and feel what we feel. We don't want to go through the detox. Yet the middle way encourages us to do just that. It encourages us to awaken the bravery that exists in everyone without exception, including you and me.

Meditation provides a way for us to train in the middle way—in staying right on the spot. We are encouraged not to judge whatever arises in our mind. In fact, we are encouraged not to even grasp whatever arises in our mind. What we usually call good or bad we simply acknowledge as thinking, without all the usual drama that goes along with right and wrong. We are instructed to let the thoughts come and go as if touching a bubble with a feather. This straightforward discipline prepares us to stop struggling and discover a fresh, unbiased state of being.

67

OBSTACLES CAN BECOME OUR TEACHERS

On the night on which he was to attain enlightenment, the Buddha sat under a tree. While he was sitting there, he was attacked by the forces of Mara (the lord of destruction). The story goes that they shot swords and arrows at him, and that their weapons turned into flowers.

What does this story mean? My understanding of it is that what we habitually regard as obstacles are not really our enemies, but rather our friends. What we call obstacles are really the way the world and our entire experience teach us where we're stuck. What may appear to be an arrow or a sword we can actually experience as a flower. Whether we experience what happens to us as obstacle and enemy or as teacher and friend depends entirely on our perception of reality. It depends on our relationship with ourselves.

68

PERFECTION IS
LIKE DEATH

We think that if we just meditated enough or jogged or ate perfect food, everything would be perfect. But from the point of view of someone who is awake, that's death. Seeking security or perfection, rejoicing in feeling confirmed and whole, self-contained and comfortable, is some kind of death. It doesn't have any fresh air. There's no room for something to come in and interrupt all that. We are killing the moment by controlling our experience. Doing this is setting ourselves up for failure, because sooner or later, we're going to have an experience we can't control: our house is going to burn down, someone we love is going to die, we're going to find out we have cancer, or somebody's going to spill tomato juice all over our white suit.

The essence of life is that it's challenging. Sometimes it is sweet, and sometimes it is bitter. Sometimes your body tenses, and sometimes it relaxes or opens. Sometimes you have a headache, and sometimes you feel 100 percent healthy. From an awakened perspective, trying to tie up all the loose ends and finally get it together is death, because it involves rejecting a lot of your basic experience. There is something aggressive about that approach to life, trying to flatten out all the rough spots and imperfections into a nice smooth ride. To be fully alive, fully human, and completely awake is to be continually thrown out of the nest. To live fully is to be always in no-man's-land, to experience each moment as completely new and fresh.

POINTING AT YOUR OWN HEART

In my office there is a scroll with Japanese calligraphy and a painting of Zen master Bodhidharma. Bodhidharma is a fat, grumpy-looking man with bushy eyebrows. He looks as if he has indigestion. The calligraphy reads, "Pointing directly at your own heart, you find Buddha."

Listening to talks about the dharma, or the teachings of Buddha, or practicing meditation is nothing other than studying ourselves. Whether we're eating or working or meditating or listening or talking, the reason that we're here in this world at all is to study ourselves. In fact, it has been said that studying ourselves provides all the books we need.

Maybe the reason there are dharma talks and books is just to encourage us to understand this simple teaching: all the wisdom about how we cause ourselves to suffer and all the wisdom about how joyful and vast and uncomplicated our minds are—these two things, the understanding of what we might call neurosis and the wisdom of unconditioned, unbiased truth—can only be found in our own experience.

SPACE PERMEATES EVERYTHING

Things happen to us all the time that open up the space. This spaciousness, this wide-open, unbiased, unprejudiced space, is inexpressibly and fundamentally good and sound. It's like the sky. Whenever you're in a hot spot or feeling uncomfortable, whenever you're caught up and don't know what to do, you can find someplace where you can go and look at the sky and experience some freshness, free of hope and fear, free of bias and prejudice, just completely open. And this is accessible to us all the time. Space permeates everything, every moment of our lives.

THE ONLY REASON WE DON'T OPEN OUR HEARTS

The only reason that we don't open our hearts and minds to other people is that they trigger confusion in us that we don't feel brave enough or sane enough to deal with. To the degree that we look clearly and compassionately at ourselves, we feel confident and fearless about looking into someone else's eyes.

72

THEY'RE UP AGAINST WHAT YOU'RE UP AGAINST

I met a young man who had been on a spiritual journey most of his life. He was awake but smug. He suffered from what's called spiritual pride. He was complaining about his girlfriend, who was having a hard time giving up smoking; the anxiety was triggering an old eating disorder. The young man said he just kept telling her to be strong, not to be so fearful, to be disciplined. And she would tell him, "I'm trying. I'm really trying. I'm doing the best I can." He was angry because it didn't seem to him that she was trying. He said, "I know I shouldn't be getting so angry about this. I know I should be more compassionate. But I just can't help it. It gets under my skin. I want to be more understanding, but she's so stuck." Then he heard himself say, "I'm trying. I'm really trying. I'm doing the best I can." When he heard himself saying *her* words, he got the message. He understood what she was up against, and it humbled him.

73

THE BIG SQUEEZE

There is often a discrepancy between our ideals and what we actually encounter. For instance, with raising children, we have a lot of good ideas, but sometimes it's very challenging to put together all the good ideas with the way our children really are, there at the breakfast table with food all over themselves. Or with meditation, have you noticed how difficult it is to actually feel emotions without getting totally swept away by them, or how difficult it is simply to cultivate friendliness toward yourself when you're feeling completely miserable or panicked or caught up?

There's a discrepancy between your inspiration and the situation as it presents itself, the immediacy of the situation. It's the rub between those two things—the squeeze between vision and reality—that causes you to grow up, to wake up to be 100 percent decent, alive, and compassionate. The big squeeze is one of the most productive places on the spiritual path.

MOVING BEYOND
SELF-PROTECTION

We think that by protecting ourselves from suffering we are being kind to ourselves. The truth is, we only become more fearful, more hardened, and more alienated. We experience ourselves as being separate from the whole. This separateness becomes like a prison for us, a prison that restricts us to our personal hopes and fears and to caring only for the people nearest to us. Curiously enough, if we primarily try to shield ourselves from discomfort, we suffer. Yet when we don't close off and we let our hearts break, we discover our kinship with all beings.

BODHICHITTA IS ALWAYS AVAILABLE

Bodhichitta, the tenderness of the awakened heart, is available in moments of caring for things, when we clean our glasses or brush our hair. It's available in moments of appreciation, when we notice the blue sky or pause and listen to the rain. It is available in moments of gratitude, when we recall a kindness or recognize another person's courage. It is available in music and dance, in art, and in poetry. Whenever we let go of holding on to ourselves and look at the world around us, whenever we connect with sorrow, whenever we connect with joy, whenever we drop our resentment and complaint, in those moments bodhichitta is here.

REMAINING STEADY

Emotional turmoil begins with an initial perception—a sight, sound, thought—which gives rise to a feeling of comfort or discomfort. This is the subtlest level of *shenpa*, the subtlest stage of getting hooked. Energetically there is a perceptible pull; it's like wanting to scratch an itch. We don't have to be advanced meditators to catch this.

This initial tug of "for" or "against" is the first place we can remain as steady as a log. Just experience the tug and relax into the restlessness of the energy, without fanning this ember with thoughts. If we stay present with the rawness of our direct experience, emotional energy can move through us without getting stuck. Of course, this isn't easy and takes practice.

THERE ARE NO PROMISES

When we are training in the art of peace, we are not given any promises that because of our noble intentions everything will be okay. In fact, there are no promises of fruition at all. Instead, we are encouraged to simply look deeply at joy and sorrow, at laughing and crying, at hoping and fearing, at all that lives and dies. We learn that what truly heals is gratitude and tenderness.

78

HOLDING ON
CAUSES SUFFERING

When we feel inadequate and unworthy, we hoard things. We are so afraid—afraid of losing, afraid of feeling even more poverty-stricken than we do already. This stinginess is extremely sad. We could look into it and shed a tear that we grasp and cling so fearfully. This holding on causes us to suffer greatly. We wish for comfort, but instead we reinforce aversion, the sense of sin, and the feeling that we are a hopeless case. The causes of aggression and fear begin to dissolve by themselves when we move past the poverty of holding back.

PATIENCE IS THE ANTIDOTE

Patience is the antidote to anger, a way to learn to love and care for whatever we meet on the path. By patience, we do not mean endurance—as in "grin and bear it." In any situation, instead of reacting suddenly, we could chew it, smell it, look at it, and open ourselves to seeing what's there. The opposite of patience is aggression—the desire to jump and move, to push against our lives, to try to fill up space. The journey of patience involves relaxing, opening to what's happening, experiencing a sense of wonder.

GAIN AND VICTORY TO OTHERS

There is a classical Tibetan Buddhist teaching that says, "Gain and victory to others, loss and defeat to myself." These words *defeat* and *victory* are so tied up with how we stay imprisoned. The real confusion is caused by not knowing that we have limitless wealth, and the confusion deepens each time we buy into this win/lose logic: if you touch me, that is defeat, and if I manage to armor myself and not be touched, that's victory.

Realizing our wealth would end our bewilderment and confusion. But the only way to do that is to let things fall apart. And that's the very thing that we dread the most—the ultimate defeat. Yet letting things fall apart would actually let fresh air into this old, stale basement of a heart that we've got.

Saying, "Loss and defeat to myself" doesn't mean to become a masochist: "Kick my head in, torture me, and dear God, may I never be happy." What it means is that you can open your heart and your mind and know what defeat feels like.

You feel too short, you have indigestion, you're too fat and too stupid. You say to yourself, "Nobody loves me, I'm always left out. I have no teeth, my hair's getting gray, I have blotchy skin, my nose runs." That all comes under the category of defeat, the defeat of ego. We're always not wanting to be who we are. However, we can never connect with our fundamental wealth as long as we are buying into this advertisement hype that we have to be someone else, that we have to smell different or have to look different.

On the other hand, when you say, "Victory to others," instead of wanting to keep it for yourself, there's the sense of sharing the whole delightful aspect of your life. You did lose some weight. You do like the way you look in the mirror. You suddenly feel like you have a nice voice, or someone falls in love with you or you fall in love with someone else. Or the seasons change and it touches your heart, or you begin to notice the snow in Vermont or the way the trees move in the wind. With anything that you want, you begin to develop the attitude of wanting to share it instead of being stingy with it or fearful around it.

THE STATE OF NOWNESS

We are given changes all the time. We can either cling to security, or we can let ourselves feel exposed, as if we had just been born, as if we had just popped out into the brightness of life and were completely naked. Maybe that sounds too uncomfortable or frightening, but on the other hand, it's our chance to realize that this mundane world is all there is, and we could see it with new eyes and at long last wake up from our ancient sleep of preconceptions.

The truth, said an ancient Chinese master, is neither like this nor like that. It is like a dog yearning over a bowl of burning oil. He can't leave it, because it is too desirable, and he can't lick it, because it is too hot. So how do we relate to that squeeze? Somehow, someone finally needs to encourage us to be inquisitive about this unknown territory and about the unanswerable question of what's going to happen next.

The state of nowness is available in that moment of squeeze. In that awkward, ambiguous moment is our own wisdom mind. Right there in the uncertainty of everyday chaos is our own wisdom mind.

ABANDON HOPE

The word in Tibetan for hope is *rewa*; the word for fear is *dokpa*. More commonly, the word *re-dok* is used, which combines the two. Hope and fear is a feeling with two sides. As long as there's one, there's always the other. This *re-dok* is the root of our pain. In the world of hope and fear, we always have to change the channel, change the temperature, change the music, because something is getting uneasy, something is getting restless, something is beginning to hurt, and we keep looking for alternatives.

In a nontheistic state of mind, abandoning hope is an affirmation, the beginning of the beginning. You could even put "Abandon hope" on your refrigerator door instead of more conventional aspirations like "Every day in every way I'm getting better and better."

Hope and fear come from feeling that we lack something; they come from a sense of poverty. We can't simply relax with ourselves. We hold on to hope, and hope robs us of the present moment.

POSITIVE SHAME

Shame is a loaded word for Westerners. Like most things, it can be seen in a positive or negative light. Negative shame is accompanied by guilt and self-denigration. It is pointless and doesn't help us even slightly. Positive shame, on the other hand, is recognizing when we've harmed ourselves or anyone else and feeling sorry for having done so. It allows us to grow wiser from our mistakes. Eventually it dawns on us that we can regret causing harm without becoming weighed down by negative shame. Just seeing the hurt and heartbreak clearly motivates us to move on. By acknowledging what we did, cleanly and compassionately, we go forward.

84

RELAX AS IT IS

We can stop struggling with what occurs and see its true face without calling it the enemy. It helps to remember that our spiritual practice is not about accomplishing anything—not about winning or losing—but about ceasing to struggle and relaxing as it is. That is what we are doing when we sit down to meditate. That attitude spreads into the rest of our lives.

GO TO THE PLACES
THAT SCARE YOU

Often in our daily lives we panic. We feel heart palpitations and stomach rumblings because we are arguing with someone or because we had a beautiful plan and it's not working out. How do we walk into those dramas? How do we deal with those demons, which are basically our hopes and fears? How do we stop struggling against ourselves? The revered Tibetan Buddhist master Machig Labdrön advised us to go to places that scare us. But how do we do that?

We're trying to learn not to split ourselves between our "good side" and our "bad side," between our "pure side" and our "impure side." The elemental struggle is with our feeling of being wrong, with our guilt and shame at what we are. That's what we have to befriend. The point is that we can dissolve the sense of dualism between us and them, between this and that, between here and there, by moving toward what we find difficult and wish to push away.

86

A PROCESS OF SURRENDERING

The journey to enlightenment involves shedding, not collecting. It's a continual process of opening and surrender, like taking off layer after layer of clothes, until we're completely naked with nothing to hide. But we can't just pretend, making a big display of disrobing, then putting everything back on when no one's looking. Our surrender has to be genuine.

OUR PREDICAMENT
IS WORKABLE

The dharma can heal our wounds, our very ancient wounds that come not from original sin but from a misunderstanding so old that we can no longer see it. The instruction is to relate compassionately with where we find ourselves and to begin to see our predicament as workable. We are stuck in patterns of grasping and fixating, which cause the same thoughts and reactions to occur again and again and again. In this way we project our world. When we see that, even if it's only for one second every three weeks, then we'll naturally discover the knack of reversing this process of making things solid, the knack of stopping the claustrophobic world as we know it, putting down our centuries of baggage, and stepping into new territory. If you ask how in the world we can do this, the answer is simple. Make the dharma personal, explore it wholeheartedly, and relax.

88

AN OPEN-ENDED APPROACH

The basic ground of compassionate action is the importance of working *with* rather than struggling *against*, and what I mean by that is working with your own unwanted, unacceptable stuff, so that when the unacceptable and unwanted appears out *there*, you relate to it based on having worked with loving-kindness for yourself. Then there is no condescension. This nondualistic approach is true to the heart because it's based on our kinship with each other. We know what to say, because we have experienced closing down, shutting off, being angry, hurt, rebellious, and so forth, and have made a relationship with those things in ourselves.

This is not about problem resolution. This is a more open-ended and courageous approach. It has to do with not knowing what will happen. It has nothing to do with wanting to get ground under your feet. It's about keeping your heart and your mind open to whatever arises, without hope of fruition. Problem-solving is based first on thinking there is a problem and second on thinking there is a solution. The concepts of problem and solution can keep us stuck in thinking that there is an enemy and a saint or a right way and a wrong way. The approach we're suggesting is more groundless than that.

THE PATH IS UNCHARTED

This path has one very distinct characteristic: it is not prefabricated. It doesn't already exist. The path that we're talking about is the moment-by-moment evolution of our experience, the moment-by-moment evolution of the world of phenomena, the moment-by-moment evolution of our thoughts and our emotions.

The path is not Route 66, destination Los Angeles. It's not as if we can take out a map and figure that this year we might make it to Gallup, New Mexico, and maybe by next year, we'll be in L.A. The path is uncharted. It comes into existence moment by moment and at the same time drops away behind us. It's like riding in a train sitting backward. We can't see where we're headed, only where we've been.

This is a very encouraging teaching, because it says that the source of wisdom is whatever is going to happen to us today. The source of wisdom is whatever is happening to us right at this very instant.

90

NOW IS THE TIME

We're always in some kind of mood. It might be sadness, it might be anger, it might be not much of anything, just a kind of blur. It might be humor or contentment. In any case, whatever it is, that's the path.

When something hurts in life, we don't usually think of it as our path or as the source of wisdom. In fact, we think that the reason we're on the path is to get rid of this painful feeling. In this way, we naively cultivate a subtle aggression against ourselves.

However, the fact is that anyone who has used the moments, days, and years of his or her life to become wiser, kinder, and more at home in the world has learned from what's happening right now. We can aspire to be kind right in the moment, to relax and open our heart and mind to what is in front of us right in the moment. Now is the time. If there's any possibility for enlightenment, it's right now, not at some future time.

LIVING AT A CROSSROADS

My teacher Trungpa Rinpoche said, "Whatever occurs in the confused mind is regarded as the path. Everything is workable. It is a fearless proclamation, the lion's roar." If we find ourselves in what seems like a rotten or painful situation and we think, "Well, how is this enlightenment?" we can just remember this notion of the path, that what seems undesirable in our lives doesn't have to put us to sleep. What seems undesirable in our lives doesn't have to trigger habitual reactions. We can let it show us where we're at and let it remind us that the teachings encourage precision and gentleness, with loving-kindness toward every moment. When we live this way, we feel frequently—maybe continuously—at a crossroads, never knowing what's ahead.

It's an insecure way to live. We often find ourselves in the middle of a dilemma—what should I do about the fact that somebody is angry with me? What should I do about the fact that I'm angry with somebody? Basically, the instruction is not to try to solve the problem but instead to use it as a question about how to let this very situation wake us up further rather than lull us into ignorance. We can use a difficult situation to encourage ourselves to take a leap, to step out into that ambiguity.

92

A MAGICAL GOLDEN KEY

Being satisfied with what we already have is a magical golden key to being alive in a full, unrestricted, and inspired way. One of the major obstacles to what is traditionally called enlightenment is resentment, feeling cheated, holding a grudge about who you are, where you are, what you are. This is why we talk so much about making friends with ourselves, because, for some reason or other, we don't feel that kind of satisfaction in a full and complete way.

Meditation is a process of lightening up, of trusting the basic goodness of what we have and who we are, and of realizing that any wisdom that exists, exists in what we already have. Our wisdom is all mixed up with what we call our neurosis. Our brilliance, our juiciness, our spiciness, is all mixed up with our craziness and our confusion, and therefore it doesn't do any good to try to get rid of our so-called negative aspects, because in that process we also get rid of our basic wonderfulness. We can lead our life so as to become more awake to who we are and what we're doing rather than trying to improve or change or get rid of who we are or what we're doing. The key is to wake up, to become more alert, more inquisitive and curious about ourselves.

TIGERS ABOVE, TIGERS BELOW

There is a story of a woman running away from tigers. She runs and runs, and the tigers are getting closer and closer. When she comes to the edge of a cliff, she sees some vines there, so she climbs down and holds on to the vines. Looking down, she sees that there are tigers below her as well. She then notices that a mouse is gnawing away at the vine to which she is clinging. She also sees a beautiful little bunch of strawberries close to her, growing out of a clump of grass. She looks up and she looks down. She looks at the mouse. Then she just takes a strawberry, puts it in her mouth, and enjoys it thoroughly.

Tigers above, tigers below. This is actually the predicament that we are always in, in terms of our birth and death. Each moment is just what it is. It might be the only moment of our life, it might be the only strawberry we'll ever eat. We could get depressed about it, or we could finally appreciate it and delight in the preciousness of every single moment of our life.

94

WE ALL HAVE WHAT IT TAKES

There is nobody on the planet, neither those whom we see as the oppressed nor those whom we see as the oppressor, who doesn't have what it takes to wake up. We all need support and encouragement to be aware of what we think, what we say, and what we do. Notice your opinions. If you find yourself becoming aggressive about your opinions, notice that. If you find yourself being nonaggressive, notice that. Cultivating a mind that does not grasp at right and wrong, you will find a fresh state of being. The ultimate cessation of suffering comes from that.

95

RAVENS IN THE WIND

How do we work with our tendency to block and to freeze and to refuse to take another step toward the unknown? If our edge is like a huge stone wall with a door in it, how do we learn to open that door and step through it again and again, so that life becomes a process of growing up, of becoming more and more fearless and flexible, more and more able to play like a raven in the wind?

Where I live on Cape Breton, Nova Scotia, I see that the wilder the weather is, the more the ravens love it. They have the time of their lives in the winter, when the wind gets much stronger and there's lots of ice and snow. They challenge the wind. They get up on the tops of the trees and they hold on with their claws and then they grab on with their beaks as well. At some point they just let go into the wind and let it blow them away. Then they play on it, they float on it. After a while, they'll go back to the tree and start over. It's a game.

Once I saw ravens in an incredible hurricane-velocity wind, grabbing each other's feet and dropping and then letting go and flying out. It was like a circus act.

The animals and the plants on Cape Breton are hardy and fearless and playful and joyful; the elements have strengthened them. In order to exist there, they have had to develop a zest for challenge and for life. As you can see, it adds up to tremendous beauty and inspiration and uplifted feeling. The same goes for us.

WHOLEHEARTED ATTENTION

When the teachings tell us to "make friends with our emotions," they mean to become more attentive and get to know them better. Being ignorant about emotions only makes matters worse; feeling guilty or ashamed of them does the same. Struggling against them is equally nonproductive. The only way to dissolve their power is with our wholehearted, intelligent attention. Only then is it possible to stay steady, connect with the underlying energy, and discover their insubstantial nature.

FEEL THE SADNESS
WITHOUT DROWNING IN IT

My teacher Chögyam Trungpa Rinpoche once said: "Hold the sadness and pain of samsara in your heart and at the same time the power and vision of the Great Eastern Sun. Then the warrior can make a proper cup of tea."

The notion of holding the sadness and pain of samsara in my heart rang true, but I realized I didn't do that; at least, I had a definite preference for the power and vision of the Great Eastern Sun—the quality of being continually awake. If you can live with the sadness of human life (what Rinpoche often called the tender heart or the genuine heart of sadness), if you can be willing to feel fully and acknowledge continually your own sadness and the sadness of life, but at the same time not be drowned in it, because you also remember the vision and power of the Great Eastern Sun, you experience balance and completeness, joining heaven and earth, joining vision and practicality.

In the Shambhala tradition we talk about men and women joining heaven and earth, but really they are already joined. There isn't any separation between samsara and the vision and power of the Great Eastern Sun. One can hold them both in one's heart, which is actually the purpose of practice. As a result of that, one can make a proper cup of tea.

98

LIVING WITHOUT AN AGENDA

Could our minds and our hearts be big enough just to hang out in that space where we're not entirely certain about who's right and who's wrong? Could we have no agenda when we walk into a room with another person, not know what to say, not make that person wrong or right? Could we see, hear, feel other people as they really are? It is powerful to practice this way, because we'll find ourselves continually rushing around to try to feel secure again—to make ourselves or them either right or wrong. But true communication can happen only in that open space.

IMPERMANENCE IS REAL

Impermanence means that the essence of life is fleeting. Some people are so skillful at their mindfulness practice that they can actually see each and every little movement of mind—changing, changing, changing. They can also feel body changing, changing, changing. It's absolutely amazing. The heart pumps blood all the time and the blood keeps going and the food gets digested and the whole thing happens. It's amazing and it's very impermanent. Every time you travel in a car, that might be the end. If you get really paranoid, impermanence can drive you crazy because you're scared to step off the curb, you're scared to go out of your house. You realize how dangerous life is. It's good to realize how dangerous it is because that makes the sense of impermanence real. It is good to realize that you will die, that death is right there on your shoulder all the time.

Many religions have meditations on death to let it penetrate our thick skulls that life doesn't last forever. It might be over in the next instant! Sometimes it's said that the end of every out-breath is actually the end; the opportunity is there to die completely. The renowned Zen master Suzuki Roshi gave the instructions, "Sit still. Don't anticipate. Just be willing to die over and over again." Let that be a reminder. Being willing to die over and over again heightens the sense of gratitude and preciousness.

Impermanence can teach you a lot about how to cheer up. Sometimes let it scare you. It is said, "Practice as if your hair were on fire." It's okay if it scares you. Fear can make you start asking a lot of questions. If it doesn't get you down, it's going to start you wondering, "What is this fear? Where did it come from? What am I scared of?" Maybe you're scared of the most exciting things you have yet to learn. Impermanence is a great reminder.

100

CONDITION YOURSELF TOWARD WAKEFULNESS

How we live is important, particularly at the level of mind. Every time you're willing to acknowledge your thoughts, let them go, and come back to the freshness of the present moment, you're sowing seeds of wakefulness in your unconscious. After a while what comes up is a more wakeful, more open thought. You're conditioning yourself toward openness rather than sleepiness. You might find yourself caught, but you can extricate yourself by how you use your mind, how you actually are willing to come back just to nowness, the immediacy of the moment. Every time you're willing to do that, you're sowing seeds for your own future, cultivating this innate fundamental wakefulness by aspiring to let go of the habitual way you proceed and do something fresh.

101

RIGHT THERE IN
THE MOMENT OF SADNESS

When you wake up in the morning and out of no-where comes the heartache of alienation and loneli-ness, could you use that as a golden opportunity? Rather than persecuting yourself or feeling that some-thing terribly wrong is happening, right there in the moment of sadness and longing, could you relax and touch the limitless space of the human heart? The next time you get a chance, experiment with this.

102

THE LAW OF KARMA

When bad feelings such as uneasiness, depression, and fear start coming up, notice how you always do the same thing. Notice how you shut down in some habitual, very old way. According to the law of karma, every action has a result. If you stay in bed all day with the covers over your head, if you overeat for the millionth time in your life, if you get drunk, if you get stoned, if it's just this habitual thing that you think is going to make you feel better, you know that's going to depress you and make you more discouraged. The older you get, the more you know how it just makes you feel more wretched.

The law of karma says, "Well, how do you want to feel tomorrow, next week, next year, five years from now, ten years from now?" It's up to you how to use your life. It doesn't mean that you have to be the best one at cheering up, or that your habitual tendencies never get the better of you. It just has to do with this sense of reminding yourself. Sometimes you can say, "Couldn't care less," but after the fourth day of lying under the sheets in your dirty, smelly clothes with your socks on, with the empty bottle next to the bed—whatever the scenario is—you say, "Maybe I should go out and buy a new shirt and take a shower and go and look at the ocean or walk in the mountains or make a nice meal or do *something* to uplift my situation, to cheer myself up." Even though we may feel very heavyhearted, instead of eating poison, we can go out and buy the best filet mignon or whatever it might be—in my case, the best peach.

103

KEEP STANDING UP

I remember my first interview with my teacher Chögyam Trungpa Rinpoche very well because I was hesitant to talk to him about what was really the problem in my life. Instead, I wasted the whole interview chattering. Every once in a while he said, "How's your meditation?" and I said, "Oh, fine," and then just chattered on. When it was almost over, I blurted out, in the last half-second, "I'm having this terrible time and I'm full of anger."

Rinpoche walked me toward the door and said, "Well, what that feels like is a big wave that comes along and knocks you down. You find yourself lying on the bottom of the ocean with your face in the sand, and even though all the sand is going up your nose and into your mouth and your eyes and ears, you stand up and you begin walking again. Then the next wave comes and knocks you down. The waves just keep coming, but each time you get knocked down, you stand up and keep walking. After a while, you'll find that the waves appear to be getting smaller."

That's how karma works. If you keep lying there, you'll drown, but you don't even have the privilege of dying. You just live with the sense of drowning all the time. So don't get discouraged and think, "Well, I was feeling depressed and I was hiding under the covers, but then I got out of bed, I took a shower. How come I'm not living in a Walt Disney movie now? I thought I was going to turn into Snow White. How come I'm not living happily ever after?" The waves just keep coming and knocking you down, but you stand up again and with some sense of rousing yourself. As Rinpoche said, "After a while, you find that the waves seem to be getting smaller." That's really what happens.

104

RECOGNIZING SUFFERING AS SUFFERING

When suffering arises in our lives, we can recognize it as suffering. When we get what we don't want, when we don't get what we do want, when we become ill, when we're getting old, when we're dying—when we see any of these things in our lives, we can recognize suffering as suffering. Then we can be curious, notice, and be mindful of our reactions to that. Again, usually we're either resentful and feel cheated somehow, or we're delighted. But whatever our reaction is, it's usually habitual. Instead, we could see the next impulse come up, and how we spin off from there. Spinning off is neither good nor bad; it's just something that happens as a reaction to the pleasure and pain of our existence. We can simply see that, without judgment or the intention to clean up our act.

ENLIGHTENMENT IS JUST THE BEGINNING

No matter where we are on the bodhisattva path, whether we are just beginning or we've practiced for years, we're always stepping further into groundlessness. Enlightenment is not the end of anything. Enlightenment, being completely awake, is just the beginning of fully entering into we know not what.

106

APPROACHING LIFE
AS AN EXPERIMENT

My teacher Trungpa Rinpoche encouraged us to lead our lives as an experiment, a suggestion that has been very important to me. When we approach life as an experiment, we're willing to try it this way and that way because, either way, we have nothing to lose.

This immense flexibility is something I learned from watching Trungpa Rinpoche. His enthusiasm enabled him to accomplish an amazing amount in his life. When some things didn't work out, Rinpoche's attitude was "no big deal." If it's time for something to flourish, it will; if it's not time, it won't.

The trick is not getting caught in hope and fear. We can put our whole heart into whatever we do; but if we freeze our attitude into for or against, we're setting ourselves up for stress. Instead, we could just go forward with curiosity, wondering where this experiment will lead.

107

ALWAYS MAINTAIN
A JOYFUL MIND

Constantly apply cheerfulness, if for no other reason than because you are on this spiritual path. Have a sense of gratitude to everything, even difficult emotions, because of their potential to wake you up.

108

WE CAN HELP
THIS TROUBLED WORLD

We all have the inborn wisdom to create a whole-some, uplifted existence for ourselves and others. We can think beyond our own little cocoon and try to help this troubled world. Not only will our friends and family benefit, but even our "enemies" will reap the blessings of peace.

If these teachings make sense to us, can we commit to them? In these times, do we really have a choice? Do we have the option of living in unconscious self-absorption? When the stakes are so high, do we have the luxury of dragging our feet?

SOURCES

1. *When Things Fall Apart*, 86–87. 2. *Start Where You Are*, 3. 3. *The Places That Scare You*, 6. 4. *Start Where You Are*, 34. 5. *When Things Fall Apart*, 10. 6. *The Places That Scare You*, 24. 7. *When Things Fall Apart*, 74. 8. *Practicing Peace in Times of War*, 65–68. 9. *The Places That Scare You*, 4–5. 10. *The Wisdom of No Escape*, 3–4.

11. *When Things Fall Apart*, 106–107. 12. *When Things Fall Apart*, 123. 13. *When Things Fall Apart*, 101. 14. *Practicing Peace in Times of War*, 73. 15. *The Wisdom of No Escape*, 3. 16. *Practicing Peace in Times of War*, 99–100. 17. *The Places That Scare You*, 3. 18. *The Places That Scare You*, 17–18, 22. 19. *Start Where You Are*, 91. 20. *Practicing Peace in Times of War*, 68–69.

21. *The Places That Scare You*, 19. 22. *When Things Fall Apart*, 38–39. 23. *The Places That Scare You*, 20. 24. *The Places That Scare You*, 19–20. 25. *The Places That Scare You*, 41. 26. *Start Where You Are*, 11–12. 27. *The Places That Scare You*, 42. 28. *The Places That Scare You*, 61–62. 29. *The Places That Scare You*, 62–63. 30. *No Time to Lose*, 236.

31. *When Things Fall Apart*, 84–85. **32.** *The Places That Scare You*, 75. **33.** *Start Where You Are*, 34–35. **34.** *The Places That Scare You*, 105–106. **35.** *Start Where You Are*, 59. **36.** *Start Where You Are*, 61–62. **37.** *Always Maintain a Joyful Mind*, 83. **38.** *Start Where You Are*, 97. **39.** *The Places That Scare You*, 67–68. **40.** *Start Where You Are*, 117.

41. *When Things Fall Apart*, 78–79. **42.** *Start Where You Are*, 123. **43.** *Practicing Peace in Times of War*, 41–42. **44.** *Start Where You Are*, 124. **45.** *Start Where You Are*, 125. **46.** *When Things Fall Apart*, 34–35. **47.** *Start Where You Are*, 132. **48.** *When Things Fall Apart*, 106. **49.** *When Things Fall Apart*, 83. **50.** *Start Where You Are*, 132–133.

51. *Start Where You Are*, 141. **52.** *When Things Fall Apart*, 91. **53.** *When Things Fall Apart*, 8. **54.** *Start Where You Are*, 14–15. **55.** *When Things Fall Apart*, 8–9. **56.** *Start Where You Are*, 47–48. **57.** *Start Where You Are*, 34. **58.** *When Things Fall Apart*, 11. **59.** *When Things Fall Apart*, 17. **60.** *Always Maintain a Joyful Mind*, 27.

61. *When Things Fall Apart*, 30. **62.** *No Time to Lose*, 259. **63.** *When Things Fall Apart*, 32. **64.** *When Things Fall Apart*, 53. **65.** *The Wisdom of No Escape*, 32. **66.** *When Things Fall Apart*, 54–55. **67.** *When Things Fall Apart*, 65. **68.** *When Things Fall Apart*, 71–72. **69.** *When Things Fall Apart*, 73. **70.** *Practicing Peace in Times of War*, 89–90.

71. *When Things Fall Apart*, 76. **72.** *Start Where You Are*, 140–141. **73.** *Start Where You Are*, 122. **74.** *When Things Fall Apart*, 87–88. **75.** *When Things Fall Apart*, 91. **76.** *No*

Time to Lose, 130. **77.** When Things Fall Apart, 100. **78.** When Things Fall Apart, 100–101. **79.** When Things Fall Apart, 104–105. **80.** Start Where You Are, 8–9.

81. When Things Fall Apart, 117–118. **82.** When Things Fall Apart, 40–41. **83.** No Time to Lose, 119–120. **84.** When Things Fall Apart, 121–122. **85.** When Things Fall Apart, 125. **86.** No Time to Lose, 61. **87.** When Things Fall Apart, 141–142. **88.** Start Where You Are, 103. **89.** When Things Fall Apart, 143–144. **90.** When Things Fall Apart, 144.

91. When Things Fall Apart, 145–146. **92.** The Wisdom of No Escape, 6–7. **93.** The Wisdom of No Escape, 25. **94.** When Things Fall Apart, 113. **95.** The Wisdom of No Escape, 54. **96.** No Time to Lose, 94. **97.** The Wisdom of No Escape, 76–77. **98.** When Things Fall Apart, 83. **99.** The Wisdom of No Escape, 102–103. **100.** The Wisdom of No Escape, 103.

101. When Things Fall Apart, 59. **102.** The Wisdom of No Escape, 104. **103.** The Wisdom of No Escape, 104–105. **104.** When Things Fall Apart, 63. **105.** The Places That Scare You, 104. **106.** No Time to Lose, 225–226. **107.** Always Maintain a Joyful Mind, 43. **108.** No Time to Lose, 360.

BIBLIOGRAPHY

Always Maintain a Joyful Mind and Other Lojong Teachings on Awakening Compassion and Fearlessness. Boston: Shambhala Publications, 2007.

No Time to Lose: A Timely Guide to the Way of the Bodhisattva. Boston: Shambhala Publications, 2007.

The Places That Scare You: A Guide to Fearlessness in Difficult Times, Shambhala Classics. Boston: Shambhala Publications, 2002.

Practicing Peace in Times of War. Boston: Shambhala Publications, 2007.

Start Where You Are: A Guide to Compassionate Living, Shambhala Classics. Boston: Shambhala Publications, 2001.

When Things Fall Apart: Heart Advice for Difficult Times, Shambhala Classics. Boston: Shambhala Publications, 2000.

The Wisdom of No Escape and the Path of Loving-Kindness, Shambhala Classics. Boston: Shambhala Publications, 2001.

ADDITIONAL RESOURCES

For information about meditation instruction or to find a practice center near you, please contact one of the following:

SHAMBHALA
1084 Tower Road
Halifax, NS B3H 2Y5
Canada
phone: (902) 425-4275
fax: (902) 423-2750
website: www.shambhala.org

SHAMBHALA EUROPE
Kartäuserwall 20
50678 Cologne
Germany
phone: 49-221-31024-00
fax: 49-221-31024-50
e-mail: europe@shambhala.org
website: www.shambhala-europe.org

Karmê Chöling
369 Patneaude Lane
Barnet, VT 05821
phone: (802) 633-2384
fax: (802) 633-3012
e-mail: karmecholing@shambhala.org
website: www.karmecholing.org

Shambhala Mountain Center
151 Shambhala Way
Red Feather Lakes, CO 80545
phone: (970) 881-2184
fax: (970) 881-2909
e-mail: info@shambhalamountain.org
website: www.shambhalamountain.org

Gampo Abbey
Pleasant Bay, NS B0E 2P0
Canada
phone: (902) 224-2752
e-mail: office@gampoabbey.org
website: www.gampoabbey.org

Naropa University is the only accredited, Buddhist-inspired university in North America. For more information, contact:

Naropa University
2130 Arapahoe Avenue
Boulder, CO 80302

phone: (303) 444-0202
website: www.naropa.edu

Audio- and videotape recordings of talks and seminars by Pema Chödrön are available from:

THE PEMA CHÖDRÖN FOUNDATION
PO Box 770630
Steamboat Springs, CO 80477
phone: (607) 738-5232
website: www.pemachodronfoundation.org

KALAPA RECORDINGS
1084 Tower Road
Halifax, NS B3H 2Y5
Canada
phone: (902) 420-1118, ext. 121
website: www.shambhalamedia.com

SOUNDS TRUE
413 South Arthur Avenue
Louisville, CO 80027
phone: (800) 333-9185
website: www.soundstrue.com

SHAMBHALA POCKET LIBRARY

THE POCKET CHÖGYAM TRUNGPA
Compiled and edited by Carolyn Rose Gimian

THE POCKET DALAI LAMA
Edited by Mary Craig

THE POCKET PEMA CHÖDRÖN
Edited by Eden Steinberg

THE POCKET RUMI
Edited by Kabir Helminski

THE POCKET THICH NHAT HANH
Compiled and edited by Melvin McLeod

THE POCKET THOMAS MERTON
Edited by Robert Inchausti